Fast Start Guide to Work from Home Jobs

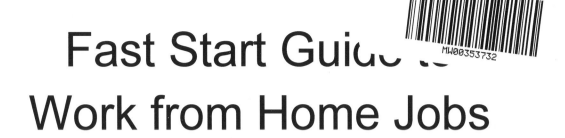

Legitimate Work from Home Job Opportunities

Diana Loera

Note – This book contains a directory of 30 companies who hire people to work remotely.   We cannot guarantee your employment.

The jobs listed are white collar jobs. In most if not all cases, you will need a computer, a separate phone line and an Internet line.

This is not a get rich quick book.

Positions may be full time or part time.

We are not responsible for broken links or companies who have ceased to operate.

Additional Books by Diana Loera

I am always looking for cool recipes and interesting topics. Below are some of my books. More are being researched and written every month.

Thank you for your interest in my books!

Summertime Sangria

Party Time Chicken Wing Recipes

Awesome Thanksgiving Leftovers Revive Guide

Best Venison Recipes

Meet Me at the County Fair – Fair Food Recipes

What is the Paleo Diet & Paleo Diet Recipe Sampler

12 Extra Special Summer Dessert Fondue Recipes

14 Extra Special Winter Holidays Fondue Recipes

USA Based Wholesale Directory 2015

Fast Start Guide to Flea Market Selling

Insider's Guide to Scrapping, Junking and Generating FAST Cash

Best Super Bowl Party Recipes

I601A – Our Journey to Ciudad Juarez

Stop Hot Flashes Now

Please visit www.LoeraPublishing.com to view all titles and descriptions or you can find my books on Amazon. Thank you.

Before We Begin

Listings in this book are shown in the Table of Contents as Work from Home Opportunity 1, Work from Home Opportunity 2 etc. The actual listing will show you the company name, a brief overview of most common work from home jobs offered by the company and contact information.

We do not include the company name in the Table of Contents as unfortunately there are people who like to use the "Look Inside" feature on Amazon to get information free. We do not think it is fair to people like yourself who purchase this book. So with that being said, we labeled each listing numerically.

At the back of the book is an index with company names to make looking up companies that caught your eye a little easier.

There is no guarantee that any of the companies listed in this directory will hire you. This book was created to help people in our down economy as many people are searching for work. Unfortunately there are a lot of people who prey on good people by creating fake jobs or demanding a fee for finding jobs – we highly suggest that you avoid those people.

The softcover edition of this book is 8 ½ by 11 inches in size. I have all my books published in this size as personally, I dislike squinting at small font in a tiny book. I have not included any photos in this book as photos do drive up the cost and I didn't see a need for photos in a book like this one.

I do suggest that before you contact any company in this book that you visit their website – which is listed with each company.

Table of Contents

Introduction

Hello! Diana Loera here. I'm the author of this neat book and of quite a few other books.

I was in the direct response (infomercial) business for over twenty years and I've seen more fake work from home scams that I can count.

I am happy to say that I didn't buy ads for hokey, undocumented phony programs and in most cases, the companies folded fairly fast thanks to Attorney General and FTC interventions.

Over the years, due to my contacts in the industry, I did come across some real, authentic work from home jobs. In some cases, I even worked with some of the companies as they offered services that my clients needed.

The work from home opportunities do exist and there are countless ones available.

Due to changes in the economy, several friends and colleagues lost their jobs. The ones who regained their financial footing fastest were the ones who accepted positions such as those in this book.

My friends did find employment and moved on from the jobs in this book but having the opportunity to become employed and also work from home helped keep them financially afloat.

I recently published several books on topics about how to make money in a down economy – USA based wholesale sources, dropshipping sources, selling at flea markets and making money scrapping/junking.

It crossed my mind that a person could do any one or all of the above and still most likely add in one of the work from home job opportunities that I was aware of – so I decided to go through my Rolodex – yes, I'm a bit old fashioned, I still have a Rolodex. It is filled with contacts and their info that I've accumulated over the past 20 plus years.

In this book, I've narrowed down my top Rolodex picks to give you 30 choices. They are listed in alphabetical order and I have no financial interest in any of them.

Before we go through the list that I am sharing with you – let's be sure you have what you will most likely need to work from home.

In most cases, you will need a separate phone line. I think most employers will ask you to have a land line, not a mobile line but you can definitely ask them yourself if there is a preferred type of line.

I am fairly comfortable saying that you will need a computer.

You will need an internet line.

You will need a designated work space in your home that is noise and distraction free.

You may need a headset – they are fairly cheap and there are a lot of options.

You will need to have a schedule in mind that you can work. In some cases, you may be able to custom tailor your work availability – within reason of course.

The benefits of course are huge – no commuting expenses, you do not need work clothes, you are not exposed to sick people during flu season and I'm sure you'll develop a list of your own personal reasons why you love working from home.

You do need discipline and perhaps even more so – family and friends need to fully understand – you are WORKING from home.

You can't stop working to take a neighbor's son to school after he missed the bus, you can't miss scheduled calls, you have a schedule (in most cases) and you have a job.

Speaking from experience as someone who is self- employed and has been for years – ensuring family and friends know you are not available even though you are home is, in my opinion, the biggest challenge at first. Eventually, they will get with the program but be prepared to remind them more than a few times.

What this book is not – there is no promise that you will land any of the jobs. However, thousands of people have landed jobs in the companies listed in this book.

These jobs are not multi- level marketing or freelance jobs (such as eLance).

While there is nothing wrong with multi -level marketing or companies such as eLance, we are on a different path in this book.

Work from Home Opportunity 1

Apex Battery
4350 Production Court
Las Vegas, NV 89115
Email: Careers@ApexSuperstores.com
Website: www.apexbattery.com

Job Overview: Apex sells an amazing array of batteries. This company allows their Customer Service Agents to work from home.
Send your resume to the email address listed above.

Work from Home Opportunity 2

Alpine Access, Inc.
1290 Broadway, Ste. 1400
Denver, CO 80203
Phone: 866.279.0585
Website: www.alpineaccess.com
Email: info@alpineacess.com

Job Overview:
Alpine Access Inc. provides customer service for its clients.
Home Based Agents work with clients' customers through telephone calls, web chats, or e-mails.
Agents work from home using their own PC, Internet access and telephone line.

Work from Home Opportunity 3

ARG InterActive, LLC
101 Stafford Street
Worcester, MA 01603
Email: info@arginteractive.com
URL: www.arginteractive.com

Job Overview: Currently looking for Regional Sales Directors – Technology Sales. Join a fast growing technology marketing company and sell to mortgage companies, banks, credit unions and real estate companies. To learn more about this opportunity please email us your resume.

Work from Home Opportunity 4

ARISE
3450 Lakeside Drive, Suite 620 – 6th Floor Miramar,
FL 33027
Website: www.arise.com
Email: admissions@admissions.arise.com

Job Overview: Arise Virtual Solutions is the leading global provider of virtual, work-at-home business process outsourcing (BPO) and crowdsourcing solutions. Visit their website for information on the hiring process.

Work from Home Opportunity 5

Bilateral Boston
PO Box 960503
Boston, MA 02196
Email: bilateralboston@hotmail.com
Website: www.bilateral.com

Based in Boston, this company hires agents for collections of past due bills.

Work from Home Opportunity 6

Blue Zebra USA
Blue Zebra Appointment Setting
25 Pequot Avenue, Suite A
Port Washington, NY 11050
Toll Free: 800.755.0094
Fax: 516.706.7040
E-mail: info@BlueZebraUSA.com
Website: www.bluezebrausa.com

Job Overview: The job that Blue Zebra USA usually has open is for appointment setting.

Work from Home Opportunity 7

Brighten Communications
455 N. McKinley St. Corona, CA 92879 909-324-3260
Website: www.brightenemployment.com

Job Overview: Lead generation callers

\

Work from Home Opportunity 8

Click N Work
Website: www.clicknwork.com

Job Overview: Click N Work delivers a range of high quality business services using teams of experienced home-based individuals. They are based in the British Virgin Islands and are a completely virtual company.

Work from Home Opportunity 9

eCallogy
90 North Main Street
Bountiful, UT 84010
Toll free: 866.eCallogy (866.322.5564)
Local: 801.463.1035
Fax: 801.463.1038
Website: www.ecallogy.com

Job Overview: Customer Service Agent– You will need an Internet connection and an extra phone line that will be used to receive calls while connected to the Internet.

This is a company that has been used by some of my clients. Utah is well known as an area where many quality call centers are located. This company is well known in the call center industry.

Work from Home Opportunity 10

Excel Sports Wear
15 Forbes Road Trafford, PA 15137
ltipton@excelsportswear.com
Website: www.excelsportswear.com
Phone: Linda Tipton 1-800-784-8857

Job Overview: The number one nationwide, custom imprint company has positions
listed on the career page. Check out their website for current openings.

Work from Home Opportunity 11

Extended Presence
Email   EPresumes@extendedpresence.com
Website: http://www.extendedpresence.com

Job Overview: Extended Presence is a U.S.-based sales outsourcing and appointment setting company located in Denver, Colorado. We take pride in our dynamic, growing, and fast-paced environment that attracts energetic, hard-working, experienced sales and marketing team players working effectively together to bring our proven services and solutions to market.

We hire experienced sales professionals who want to utilize their well- honed expertise but looking to reach even higher levels of inside sales tele-prospecting proficiency. Our combination of unparalleled experience, comprehensive capabilities across multiple industries and business functions, and extensive research on the world's most successful companies enables us to collaborate with our B2B clients to help them improve their sales pipeline opportunities.

Work from Home Opportunity 12

Focus Infomatics, Inc.
500 West Cummings Park, Suite 6100
Woburn, MA 01801
Phone: 877-313-8569
Fax: 781-970-5304
Email: jobs@focusinfomatics.com
Website: www.nuance-nts.com or www.focusinfomatics.com

Job Overview: Focus Infomatics, Inc. is a part of Nuance Transcription Services.

Focus Infomatics, Inc. is currently hiring US domestic MT-Editors with a minimum of 2 years of recent acute care experience to work with advanced voice recognition technology.

If interested, you can apply via their website.

Work from Home Opportunity 13

IVMS Video Home Tours
6400 Shafer Court, Suite 200
Rosemont, IL 60018
Job Info: www.vht.com/about/careers.aspx

Job Overview: This Illinois based company currently had several open positions including photography, marketing and sales leads opportunities that allow you to work from home.

In reviewing their website, they also have a variety of other jobs listed in January 2015 so it is definitely worth checking out their web site for updates on open positions.

Work from Home Opportunity 14

J. Lodge
12298 Matterhorn Rd.
Fort Myers, FL 33913
Toll Free: 888-354-5050
General Email: info@jlodge.com
Website: www.jlodge.com

Job Overview: Quality Analysts are to perform quality assurance audits on phone calls, emails and chats.

The analysts will review and grade customer contact events for technical accuracy, compliance to policies and procedures and observable soft skills.

The analyst may also provide measurements to help gauge the customers overall level of satisfaction with the contact event.

All qualified J. Lodge Analysts are permitted to work from home offices.

Work from Home Opportunity 15

Latus Point
1595 Peachtree Parkway STE 204-394
Cumming, GA 30041
Email: sales@latuspoint.com
Website: www.latuspoint.com
Phone: 404-915-3870
Fax: 678-731-1581

Job Overview: IT Sales positions

Work from Home Opportunity 16

LiveOps, Inc.
3340 Hillview Avenues
Palo Alto, California 94304
Phone: 650.461.1000
Fax: 650.745.3756
Website: www.liveops.com
Apply: http://www.liveops.com/become_agents.html

Job Overview:
LiveOps is leading the revolution in remote agent tele-services. They have built the largest network of home-based tele-services agents in the nation.

I have lost count of how many times that I have worked with LiveOps over the years. I will say this – I have never talked with an employee there who did not like their job. I have set up countless infomercial clients with their call centers over the years and every time I have been treated very good by this group.

Work from Home Opportunity 17

Metavize, Inc.
2000 Alameda de las Pulgas Suite 125
San Mateom CA 94403
Phone: 650-345-5153
Fax: 650-345-3788
Email: don@metavize.com
Website: www.metavize.com

Job Overview: Sales for IT and security software products. The site link above now points to Untangled.com but if you have a solid IT sales background, it may be worth querying this company regarding any open positions.

Work from Home Opportunity 18

Nolo Press Human Resources
950 Parker Street Berkeley, CA 94710
Website: http://www.nolo.com/jobs.html

Job Overview: This information company has careers that allow you to have a work at home base.

You may have seen one of the Nolo books if you have ever researched contracts or other business topics. I own numerous Nolo books and have always been pleased with my purchases.

If you like working with information, this company is worth a look. I looked at their site and there are numerous listings at this time. If there are not many listing when you look, then check back. Nolo is very well established and respected in the industry.

Work from Home Opportunity 19

NROTC
111 North Stuart Street
Baltimore, Maryland
Website: www.nrotc.org
Phone: 410-687-3568
Fax: 410-687-3568

Job Overview: In Home Telemarketers in all 50 states. NROTC is the shortened name for the National Remember Our Troops Campaign.

Work from Home Opportunity 20

NTI Central
Address: 1505 Commonwealth Ave
Boston, MA 02135
Email: info@nticentral.org
Website: http://nticentral.org

Job Overview: National Telecommuting Institute (NTI) is a unique/job-matching organization pioneering the development of telework jobs for those with disabilities.

Work from Home Opportunity 21

Pearson Technology
Pearson Human Resources
2510 North Dodge St
Iowa City, IA 52245
Phone: 1-888-655-6495 (select option 2 for Human Resources)
Website: http://flexiblescoring-sat.pearson.com/

Job Overview: Currently hiring Scorers- These individuals will read and score high school level essays with a user-friendly online scoring system to allow accurate and effective essay scoring,

Must meet the following qualifications:
Hold a Bachelor's degree or higher
Reside in the continental United States, including Alaska or Hawaii
or authorized to work in the U.S.

Work from Home Opportunity 22

Pomeroy Solutions
U.S Headquarters
1020 Petersburg Road
Hebron, KY 41048
859-586-0600
Toll Free 800-846-872
Website: www.pomeroy.com

Job Overview: We're looking for dedicated, hard-working individuals who will help us achieve our goal of being the best IT provider in the markets we serve. Our North American corporate office is located on a 20-acre campus in the greater Cincinnati area, but we hire for projects throughout the United States and Canada.

We pride ourselves on our ability to hire top talent, promote people within the company and offer both technical and soft-skills training to our employees.

Pomeroy offers a competitive salary and benefits program, including:

Medical, dental and vision insurance
401(k) investing
Flexible spending accounts
Short- and long-term disability
Employer-paid life insurance

Pomeroy offer opportunities that will allow workers to telecommute from anywhere in the US.

Work from Home Opportunity 23

Progent Corporation
560 South Winchester Blvd 5th Floor
San Jose, CA 95128
Phone: 408-240-9400
Fax: 408-240-9450
Website: www.progent.com

Job Overview: Jobs for IT Engineers and Consultants.

Work from Home Opportunity 24

Service 800
2190 West Wayzata Blvd.
Minneapolis, MN 55356-0800
Toll free: 800-475-3747
Local: 952-475-3747
Fax: 952-475-3773
Website: www.service800.com

Job Overview: Service 800 is looking for motivated individuals who are willing to work from home as an employee of Service 800 Inc.

You must be bright, personable and can articulate well verbally and in written form.

You will be conducting interviews with customers who have recently had a service experience.

Previous customer service experience, computer knowledge and telephone skills are mandatory.

Work from Home Opportunity 25

Teachers-Teachers.com
Email: jobs@teachers-teacher.com
Website: www.teachers-teachers.com

Job Overview: This is a really cool site that offers job listings from all over the US for public and private schools. While most listings appear to be teaching and coaching related, there are also support staff jobs listed too. There are also sales jobs which can be done from home. If you do not see a job that fits what you are looking for on this site, you may want to check back as it is constantly be updated since it lists opportunities from all over the US.

Work from Home Opportunity 26

Tele Reach Corporate,
14173 Northwest Freeway, Unit 192
Houston, Texas 77040
Email: traciec@telereach.com
Phone: (713) 956-8700
Website: www.telereach

Job Overview: In business since 1996, Tele Reach Corporate, based in Houston, is a business development, appointment setting, lead generation and information gathering company that offers home based employment.

Work from Home Opportunity 27

Ubiqus
New York 22 Cortlandt Street Suite 802
New York, NY 10007
Tel: 212 227 2440
Toll-free: 800 221 7242
Fax: 212 227 7524
Email: infousa@ubiqus.com
Website: http://www.ubiqus.com/

Job Overview:

This company has come up a few times in my Rolodex. They offer translation and transcription services.

If you speak a second language and/or are a fast and accurate transcriptionist – this company may be worth a look.

Work from Home Opportunity 28

Ver-A-Fast Corporation
20545 Center Ridge Road, Suite 300 Rocky River,
Ohio 44116
Toll Free: (800) 587-4052 or (440) 331-9962 ext. 3202
Website: http://www.verafast.net/job_opportunities.htm

Job Overview: How would you like to work from the comfort of your own home; enjoy convenient hours; use your personal computer to help us meet our clients' needs?

Sound too good to be true?

Think there's a catch? Well there isn't.

We work primarily with the newspaper industry. Our customer service representatives work from their homes making customer service calls for our newspaper clients. In many instances, we are checking on the customer's service and reporting back to the newspaper so they can take appropriate action.

Work from Home Opportunity 29

West Corporation
11808 Miracle Hills Omaha, NE 68154
Toll Free: 1-800-762-3800
Website: http://apply.westathome.com/

Job Overview: I have worked with West since the early 1990's. I've rolled out client scripts and worked with West agents on the phone and in person at their call center. If you are interested in taking calls from home for a variety of products and services – West should be on your consideration list.

Work from Home Opportunity 30

World Singles LLC
Telephone: +1-301-294-0131
Fax: +1-202-318-0432
jobs@worldsingles.com
Website: www.worldsingles.com

Job Overview: This company hires Database Engineers and Web Programmers and allows them to work from their home offices.

Made in the USA
Middletown, DE
29 June 2018